CHINESE
HOROSCOPES
FOR
LOVERS

The Pig

LORI REID

illustrated by
PAUL COLLICUTT

ELEMENT BOOKS

Shaftesbury, Dorset • Rockport, Massachusetts • Brisbane, Queensland

© Lori Reid 1996

First published in Great Britain in 1996 by

ELEMENT BOOKS LIMITED

Shaftesbury, Dorset SP7 8BP

Published in the USA in 1996 by

ELEMENT BOOKS, INC.

PO Box 830, Rockport, MA 01966

Published in Australia in 1996 by

ELEMENT BOOKS LIMITED

for JACARANDA WILEY LIMITED

33 Park Road, Milton, Brisbane 4064

The moral right of the author has been asserted.

Designed and created by

THE BRIDGEWATER BOOK COMPANY

Art directed by *Peter Bridgewater*

Designed by *Angela Neal*

Picture research by *Vanessa Fletcher*

Edited by *Gillian Delaforce*

Printed and bound in Great Britain by
BPC Paulton Books Ltd

British Library Cataloguing in Publication data available

Library of Congress Cataloging in Publication data available

ISBN 1-85230-772-2

Contents

8

*Why are
some people
lucky in
love and
others not?*

Chinese Astrology

SOME PEOPLE fall in love and, as the fairy tales go, live happily ever after. Others fall in love – again and again, make the same mistakes every time and never form a lasting relationship. Most of us come between these two extremes, and

some people form remarkably successful unions while others make spectacular disasters of their personal lives. Why are some people lucky in love while others have the odds stacked against them?

ANIMAL NAMES

According to the philosophy of the Far East, luck has very little to do with it. The answer, the philosophers say, lies with 'the Animal that hides in our hearts'. This Animal, of which there are 12, forms part of the complex art of Chinese Astrology. Each year of a 12-year cycle is attributed an Animal sign, whose characteristics are said to influence worldly events as well as the personality and fate of each living thing that comes under its dominion. The 12 Animals run in sequence, beginning with the Rat and followed by the Ox, Tiger, Rabbit, Dragon, Snake, Horse, Sheep, Monkey, Rooster, Dog and last, but not least, the Pig. Being born in the Year of the Ox, for example, is simply a way of describing what you're like, physically and psychologically. And this is quite different from someone who, for instance, is born in the Year of the Snake.

豬

9

*The 12
Animals
of Chinese
Astrology.*

RELATIONSHIPS

These Animal names are merely the tip of the
ice-berg, considering the complexity of the whole
subject. Yet such are the richness and wisdom of Chinese
Astrology that understanding the principles behind the year in
which you were born will give you powerful insights into your
own personality. The system is very specific about which Animals
are compatible and which are antagonistic and this tells us
whether our relationships will be successful. Marriages are made
in heaven, so the saying goes. The heavens, according to Chinese
beliefs, can point the way. The rest is up to us.

10

Year Chart and Birth Dates

UNLIKE THE WESTERN CALENDAR, which is based on the Sun, the Oriental year is based on the movement of the Moon, which means that New Year's Day does not fall on a fixed date. This Year Chart, taken from the Chinese Perpetual Calendar, lists the dates on which each year begins and ends together with its Animal ruler for the year. In addition, the Chinese believe that the tangible world is composed of 5 elements, each slightly adapting the characteristics of the Animal signs. These elemental influences are also given here. Finally, the aspect, that is, whether the year is characteristically Yin (-) or Yang (+), is also listed.

The Western calendar is based on the Sun; the Oriental on the Moon.

YIN AND YANG

Yin and Yang are the terms given to the dynamic complementary forces that keep the universe in balance and which are the central principles behind life. Yin is all that is considered negative, passive, feminine, night, the Moon, while Yang is considered positive, active, masculine, day, the Sun.

11

Year	From – To		Animal sign	Element	Aspect
1900	31 Jan 1900 – 18 Feb 1901		Rat	Metal	+ Yang
1901	19 Feb 1901 – 7 Feb 1902		Ox	Metal	– Yin
1902	8 Feb 1902 – 28 Jan 1903		Tiger	Water	+ Yang
1903	29 Jan 1903 – 15 Feb 1904		Rabbit	Water	– Yin
1904	16 Feb 1904 – 3 Feb 1905		Dragon	Wood	+ Yang
1905	4 Feb 1905 – 24 Jan 1906		Snake	Wood	– Yin
1906	25 Jan 1906 – 12 Feb 1907		Horse	Fire	+ Yang
1907	13 Feb 1907 – 1 Feb 1908		Sheep	Fire	– Yin
1908	2 Feb 1908 – 21 Jan 1909		Monkey	Earth	+ Yang
1909	22 Jan 1909 – 9 Feb 1910		Rooster	Earth	– Yin
1910	10 Feb 1910 – 29 Jan 1911		Dog	Metal	+ Yang
1911	30 Jan 1911 – 17 Feb 1912		Pig	Metal	– Yin
1912	18 Feb 1912 – 5 Feb 1913		Rat	Water	+ Yang
1913	6 Feb 1913 – 25 Jan 1914		Ox	Water	– Yin
1914	26 Jan 1914 – 13 Feb 1915		Tiger	Wood	+ Yang
1915	14 Feb 1915 – 2 Feb 1916		Rabbit	Wood	– Yin
1916	3 Feb 1916 – 22 Jan 1917		Dragon	Fire	+ Yang
1917	23 Jan 1917 – 10 Feb 1918		Snake	Fire	– Yin
1918	11 Feb 1918 – 31 Jan 1919		Horse	Earth	+ Yang
1919	1 Feb 1919 – 19 Feb 1920		Sheep	Earth	– Yin
1920	20 Feb 1920 – 7 Feb 1921		Monkey	Metal	+ Yang
1921	8 Feb 1921 – 27 Jan 1922		Rooster	Metal	– Yin
1922	28 Jan 1922 – 15 Feb 1923		Dog	Water	+ Yang
1923	16 Feb 1923 – 4 Feb 1924		Pig	Water	– Yin
1924	5 Feb 1924 – 24 Jan 1925		Rat	Wood	+ Yang
1925	25 Jan 1925 – 12 Feb 1926		Ox	Wood	– Yin
1926	13 Feb 1926 – 1 Feb 1927		Tiger	Fire	+ Yang
1927	2 Feb 1927 – 22 Jan 1928		Rabbit	Fire	– Yin
1928	23 Jan 1928 – 9 Feb 1929		Dragon	Earth	+ Yang
1929	10 Feb 1929 – 29 Jan 1930		Snake	Earth	– Yin
1930	30 Jan 1930 – 16 Feb 1931		Horse	Metal	+ Yang
1931	17 Feb 1931 – 5 Feb 1932		Sheep	Metal	– Yin
1932	6 Feb 1932 – 25 Jan 1933		Monkey	Water	+ Yang
1933	26 Jan 1933 – 13 Feb 1934		Rooster	Water	– Yin
1934	14 Feb 1934 – 3 Feb 1935		Dog	Wood	+ Yang
1935	4 Feb 1935 – 23 Jan 1936		Pig	Wood	– Yin

12

Year	From – To		Animal sign	Element	Aspect	
1936	24 Jan 1936 – 10 Feb 1937		Rat	Fire	+	Yang
1937	11 Feb 1937 – 30 Jan 1938		Ox	Fire	–	Yin
1938	31 Jan 1938 – 18 Feb 1939		Tiger	Earth	+	Yang
1939	19 Feb 1939 – 7 Feb 1940		Rabbit	Earth	–	Yin
1940	8 Feb 1940 – 26 Jan 1941		Dragon	Metal	+	Yang
1941	27 Jan 1941 – 14 Feb 1942		Snake	Metal	–	Yin
1942	15 Feb 1942 – 4 Feb 1943		Horse	Water	+	Yang
1943	5 Feb 1943 – 24 Jan 1944		Sheep	Water	–	Yin
1944	25 Jan 1944 – 12 Feb 1945		Monkey	Wood	+	Yang
1945	13 Feb 1945 – 1 Feb 1946		Rooster	Wood	–	Yin
1946	2 Feb 1946 – 21 Jan 1947		Dog	Fire	+	Yang
1947	22 Jan 1947 – 9 Feb 1948		Pig	Fire	–	Yin
1948	10 Feb 1948 – 28 Jan 1949		Rat	Earth	+	Yang
1949	29 Jan 1949 – 16 Feb 1950		Ox	Earth	–	Yin
1950	17 Feb 1950 – 5 Feb 1951		Tiger	Metal	+	Yang
1951	6 Feb 1951 – 26 Jan 1952		Rabbit	Metal	–	Yin
1952	27 Jan 1952 – 13 Feb 1953		Dragon	Water	+	Yang
1953	14 Feb 1953 – 2 Feb 1954		Snake	Water	–	Yin
1954	3 Feb 1954 – 23 Jan 1955		Horse	Wood	+	Yang
1955	24 Jan 1955 – 11 Feb 1956		Sheep	Wood	–	Yin
1956	12 Feb 1956 – 30 Jan 1957		Monkey	Fire	+	Yang
1957	31 Jan 1957 – 17 Feb 1958		Rooster	Fire	–	Yin
1958	18 Feb 1958 – 7 Feb 1959		Dog	Earth	+	Yang
1959	8 Feb 1959 – 27 Jan 1960		Pig	Earth	–	Yin
1960	28 Jan 1960 – 14 Feb 1961		Rat	Metal	+	Yang
1961	15 Feb 1961 – 4 Feb 1962		Ox	Metal	–	Yin
1962	5 Feb 1962 – 24 Jan 1963		Tiger	Water	+	Yang
1963	25 Jan 1963 – 12 Feb 1964		Rabbit	Water	–	Yin
1964	13 Feb 1964 – 1 Feb 1965		Dragon	Wood	+	Yang
1965	2 Feb 1965 – 20 Jan 1966		Snake	Wood	–	Yin
1966	21 Jan 1966 – 8 Feb 1967		Horse	Fire	+	Yang
1967	9 Feb 1967 – 29 Jan 1968		Sheep	Fire	–	Yin
1968	30 Jan 1968 – 16 Feb 1969		Monkey	Earth	+	Yang
1969	17 Feb 1969 – 5 Feb 1970		Rooster	Earth	–	Yin
1970	6 Feb 1970 – 26 Jan 1971		Dog	Metal	+	Yang
1971	27 Jan 1971 – 15 Jan 1972		Pig	Metal	–	Yin

豬

豬

13

Year	From – To	Animal sign	Element	Aspect	
1972	16 Jan 1972 – 2 Feb 1973	Rat	Water	+	Yang
1973	3 Feb 1973 – 22 Jan 1974	Ox	Water	–	Yin
1974	23 Jan 1974 – 10 Feb 1975	Tiger	Wood	+	Yang
1975	11 Feb 1975 – 30 Jan 1976	Rabbit	Wood	–	Yin
1976	31 Jan 1976 – 17 Feb 1977	Dragon	Fire	+	Yang
1977	18 Feb 1977 – 6 Feb 1978	Snake	Fire	–	Yin
1978	7 Feb 1978 – 27 Jan 1979	Horse	Earth	+	Yang
1979	28 Jan 1979 – 15 Feb 1980	Sheep	Earth	–	Yin
1980	16 Jan 1980 – 4 Feb 1981	Monkey	Metal	+	Yang
1981	5 Feb 1981 – 24 Jan 1982	Rooster	Metal	–	Yin
1982	25 Jan 1982 – 12 Feb 1983	Dog	Water	+	Yang
1983	13 Feb 1983 – 1 Feb 1984	Pig	Water	–	Yin
1984	2 Feb 1984 – 19 Feb 1985	Rat	Wood	+	Yang
1985	20 Feb 1985 – 8 Feb 1986	Ox	Wood	–	Yin
1986	9 Feb 1986 – 28 Jan 1987	Tiger	Fire	+	Yang
1987	29 Jan 1987 – 16 Feb 1988	Rabbit	Fire	–	Yin
1988	17 Feb 1988 – 5 Feb 1989	Dragon	Earth	+	Yang
1989	6 Feb 1989 – 26 Jan 1990	Snake	Earth	–	Yin
1990	27 Jan 1990 – 14 Feb 1991	Horse	Metal	+	Yang
1991	15 Feb 1991 – 3 Feb 1992	Sheep	Metal	–	Yin
1992	4 Feb 1992 – 22 Jan 1993	Monkey	Water	+	Yang
1993	23 Jan 1993 – 9 Feb 1994	Rooster	Water	–	Yin
1994	10 Feb 1994 – 30 Jan 1995	Dog	Wood	+	Yang
1995	31 Jan 1995 – 18 Feb 1996	Pig	Wood	–	Yin
1996	19 Feb 1996 – 7 Feb 1997	Rat	Fire	+	Yang
1997	8 Feb 1997 – 27 Jan 1998	Ox	Fire	–	Yin
1998	28 Jan 1998 – 15 Feb 1999	Tiger	Earth	+	Yang
1999	16 Feb 1999 – 4 Feb 2000	Rabbit	Earth	–	Yin
2000	5 Feb 2000 – 23 Jan 2001	Dragon	Metal	+	Yang
2001	24 Jan 2001 – 11 Feb 2002	Snake	Metal	–	Yin
2002	12 Feb 2002 – 31 Jan 2003	Horse	Water	+	Yang
2003	1 Feb 2003 – 21 Jan 2004	Sheep	Water	–	Yin
2004	22 Jan 2004 – 8 Feb 2005	Monkey	Wood	+	Yang
2005	9 Feb 2005 – 28 Jan 2006	Rooster	Wood	–	Yin
2006	29 Jan 2006 – 17 Feb 2007	Dog	Fire	+	Yang
2007	18 Feb 2007 – 6 Feb 2008	Pig	Fire	–	Yin

14

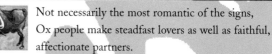

Introducing the Animals

| THE RAT | ♥ ♥ ♥ DRAGON, MONKEY | ✖ HORSE |

Outwardly cool, Rats are passionate lovers with depths of feeling that others don't often recognize. Rats are very self-controlled.

| THE OX | ♥ ♥ ♥ SNAKE, ROOSTER | ✖ SHEEP |

Not necessarily the most romantic of the signs, Ox people make steadfast lovers as well as faithful, affectionate partners.

| THE TIGER | ♥ ♥ ♥ HORSE, DOG | ✖ MONKEY |

Passionate and sensual, Tigers are exciting lovers. Flirty when young, once committed they make stable partners and keep their sexual allure.

| THE RABBIT | ♥ ♥ ♥ SHEEP, PIG | ✖ ROOSTER |

Gentle, emotional and sentimental, Rabbits make sensitive lovers. They are shrewd and seek a partner who offers security.

| THE DRAGON | ♥ ♥ ♥ RAT, MONKEY | ✖ DOG |

Dragon folk get as much stimulation from mind-touch as they do through sex. A partner on the same wave-length is essential.

| THE SNAKE | ♥ ♥ ♥ OX, ROOSTER | ✖ PIG |

Deeply passionate, strongly sexed but not aggressive, snakes are attracted to elegant, refined partners. But they are deeply jealous and possessive.

♥ ♥ ♥ *COMPATIBLE*   ✖ *INCOMPATIBLE*

15

| THE HORSE | ♥ ♥ ♥ TIGER, DOG | ✖ RAT |

For horse-born folk love is blind. In losing their hearts, they lose their heads and make several mistakes before finding the right partner.

| THE SHEEP | ♥ ♥ ♥ RABBIT, PIG | ✖ OX |

Sheep-born people are made for marriage. Domesticated home-lovers, they find emotional satisfaction with a partner who provides security.

| THE MONKEY | ♥ ♥ ♥ DRAGON, RAT | ✖ TIGER |

Clever and witty, Monkeys need partners who will keep them stimulated. Forget the 9 to 5 routine, these people need *pizzazz*.

| THE ROOSTER | ♥ ♥ ♥ OX, SNAKE | ✖ RABBIT |

The Rooster's stylish good looks guarantee they will attract many suitors. They are level-headed and approach relationships coolly.

| THE DOG | ♥ ♥ ♥ TIGER, HORSE | ✖ DRAGON |

A loving, stable relationship is an essential component in the lives of Dogs. Once they have found their mate, they remain faithful for life.

| THE PIG | ♥ ♥ ♥ RABBIT, SHEEP | ✖ SNAKE |

These are sensual hedonists who enjoy lingering love-making between satin sheets. Caviar and champagne go down very nicely too.

16

The Pig Personality

YEARS OF THE PIG

1911 ★ 1923 ★ 1935 ★ 1947 ★ 1959
1971 ★ 1983 ★ 1995 ★ 2007

BORN WITH A NATURALLY PATIENT and cheerful disposition, you're an outgoing, jovial character who is able to brighten and jolly along anyone you meet. You're by nature kind and caring, with an easy-going manner which belies your resilience and tenacity. Honest as the day is long, you expect others to be just as sincere as you are yourself – which contributes to your charm but also gives you a trusting, almost wide-eyed naivety when it comes to your dealings with others.

PIG FACTS

Twelfth in order ★ *Chinese name – Zhu* ★ *Sign of honesty*
★ *Hour – 9PM – 10.59PM* ★ *Month – November* ★
★ *Western counterpart – Scorpio* ★

CHARACTERISTICS

♥ *Sincerity* ♥ *Gregariousness* ♥ *Diligence* ♥ *Generosity*
♥ *Obligingness* ♥ *Unpretentiousness*

✖ *Naivety* ✖ *Materialism* ✖ *Superficiality* ✖ *Pigheadedness*
✖ *Gullibility* ✖ *Laziness*

豬

17

*Whether doting on grandchildren or lending a helping
hand, big-hearted Pigs give without stinting.*

HELPFUL PIG

Always considerate, you're ready to drop whatever you're doing
and run to the assistance of anyone in need. Because you're so
generous you give willingly of your time and money to help those
less fortunate than yourself. Sometimes people take advantage of
your good nature but you seldom bear a grudge, and give others
chance after chance to redeem themselves. However, if put upon
too often, even you will draw the line. A Pig in a rage is not a
pretty sight!

*In their
dreams, all
Pigs are
unashamed
sybarites.*

LA DOLCE VITA

Arch-sensualist that you are, you adore the good things in life and
have a special fondness for the *dolce vita*. Creature comforts are
essential to your well-being and, if the truth be known, it's a
pampered life of luxury that you crave.

Your Hour of Birth

WHILE YOUR YEAR OF BIRTH describes your fundamental character, the Animal governing the actual hour in which you were born describes your outer temperament, how people see you or the picture you present to the outside world. Note that each Animal rules over two consecutive hours. Also note that these are GMT standard times and that adjustments need to be made if you were born during Summer or daylight saving time.

11PM – 12.59AM ★ RAT

Pleasant, sociable, easy to get on with. An active, confident, busy person – and a bit of a busybody to boot.

1AM – 2.59AM ★ OX

Level-headed and down-to-earth, you come across as knowledgeable and reliable – sometimes, though, a bit biased.

3AM – 4.59AM ★ TIGER

Enthusiastic and self-assured, people see you as a strong and positive personality – at times a little over-exuberant.

5AM – 6.59AM ★ RABBIT

You're sensitive and shy and don't project your real self to the world. You feel you have to put on an act to please others.

7AM – 8.59AM ★ DRAGON

Independent and interesting, you present a picture of someone who is quite out of the ordinary.

9AM – 10.59AM ★ SNAKE

You can be a bit difficult to fathom and, because you appear so controlled, people either take to you instantly, or not at all.

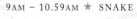

11AM – 12.59PM ★ HORSE

 Open, cheerful and happy-go-lucky is the picture you always put across to others. You're an extrovert and it generally shows.

1PM – 2.59PM ★ SHEEP

Your unassuming nature won't allow you to foist yourself upon others so people see you as quiet and retiring – but eminently sensible, though.

3PM – 4.59PM ★ MONKEY

Lively and talkative, that twinkle in your eye will guarantee you make friends wherever you go.

5PM – 6.59PM ★ ROOSTER

 There's something rather stylish in your approach that gives people an impression of elegance and glamour. But you don't suffer fools gladly.

7PM – 8.59PM ★ DOG

Some people see you as steady and reliable, others as quiet and graceful and others still as dull and unimaginative. It all depends who you're with at the time.

9PM – 10.59PM ★ PIG

Your laid-back manner conceals a depth of interest and intelligence that doesn't always come through at first glance.

Your hour of birth describes your outer temperament.

20

The Pig Lover

You adore the whole physicality of intimate relationships, the thrill of skin against skin, the excitement and voluptuousness of making love, of giving and receiving pleasure with your mate. Spending a whole rainy Sunday in bed together is your idea of bliss.

UNLIKE IN THE WESTERN WORLD where 'pig' is a term of abuse, in the Orient the pig is regarded as a symbol of contentment and good fortune. And indeed, in general you can be described as happy, good-natured and satisfied with your lot. Of all the Animals in the Chinese horoscope, you are perhaps the one who is the most suited to married life and you function at your best when attached to a doting partner. Warm and loving, you give your affection generously, adoring the physical proximity of another body to cuddle up to.

Affectionate, relaxed, hands–on togetherness is what Pigs adore.

HEALTHY LIBIDO

It's said that Pig-born folk possess healthy libidos, that they revel in sex and can be physically demanding between the sheets. Many are promiscuous in their younger years and some can develop a rather earthy or bawdy side to their natures tending, if uncontrolled, towards lasciviousness.

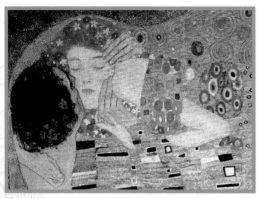

The Kiss
GUSTAV KLIMT 1862–1918

LOYAL PARTNER

It may not be the grand passion that drives you into marriage, but more the promise of companionship and security. When you decide to settle down you make a loyal partner, caring and considerate of the one you love.

You seek harmony in a relationship and avoid confrontations like the plague, preferring to flow with the tide. As you sink into your hot bath – all Pigs adore the sensual luxury of bathing – you can take a deep breath and count your blessings.

Pigs find it easy to abandon themselves to innocent sensual pleasure.

22

In Your Element

ALTHOUGH YOUR SIGN recurs every 12 years, each generation is slightly modified by one of 5 elements. If you were born under the Metal influence your character, emotions and behaviour would show significant variations from an individual born under one of the other elements. Check the Year Chart for your ruling element and discover what effects it has upon you.

THE METAL PIG ★ 1911 AND 1971

Strong and assertive, you're a passionate creature who puts one hundred per cent effort into everything you do – especially your relationships. At work you're cheerful and industrious, to your partner you're faithful and true, and though explosive at times, you're worth your weight in gold.

THE WATER PIG ★ 1923 AND 1983

Infinitely malleable and too trusting for your own good, you are, nevertheless, adept at dealing with people. Although easily influenced you can be highly persuasive with others. Helpful and kind, you like to be of service. A keen business man or woman, you're at your happiest in the bosom of your family.

THE WOOD PIG ★ 1935 AND 1995

Subtlety and diplomacy stand you in good stead when handling other people. Characteristically big-hearted and generous, you never stint in giving time and money to worthwhile and charitable causes. Understanding and co-operative, you work well with others and are especially good at dealing with people.

THE FIRE PIG ★ 1947 AND 2007

Adventurous, bold and dynamic, you're capable of outstanding acts of heroism for, once you have an objective, it's almost impossible to deflect you from your course. Because you're impulsive, you take risks which sometimes pay off and sometimes don't. Above all else, you're an out-and-out pleasure-seeker.

THE EARTH PIG ★ 1959

Easy-going and sensible, you're happy with your family, your circumstances and your life. Patient and reliable, Earth bestows upon you a practical bent so that you take a methodical approach to organizing your affairs. A tendency to over-indulge needs to be curbed.

24

*Rencontre
du Soir
(detail)*
THEOPHILE-
ALEXANDRE
STEINLEN
1859–1923

A Pig and
a Rabbit
make a
very close
couple.

Partners in Love

THE CHINESE are very definite about which animals are compatible with each other and which are antagonistic. So find out if you're truly suited to your partner.

PIG + RAT
★ *A roller-coaster of a relationship. Terrific attraction and companionship between you, but watch those bills!*

PIG + OX
★ *Sexual attraction and some shared attitudes can produce harmony and contentment if both try hard.*

PIG + TIGER
★ *Friendship and shared interests bode well for your union.*

PIG + RABBIT
★ *Warm, comfortable and close. Star-tipped for enduring love.*

PIG + DRAGON
★ *A caring, sharing and deeply loving partnership.*

PIG + SNAKE
★ *Alas, little common ground.*

PIG + HORSE
★ *A laid-back sort of affair, but who would remember to pay the bills or stock the larder?*

Eiaha chipa
PAUL GAUGUIN 1848–1903

LOVE PARTNERS AT A GLANCE

Pig with:	Tips on Togetherness	Compatibility
Rat	great happiness and good friends	♥♥♥
Ox	worth persisting at	♥♥
Tiger	good humour keeps you smiling thro'	♥♥♥
Rabbit	shared togetherness	♥♥♥♥
Dragon	sooooo comfy	♥♥♥
Snake	deep divisions	♥
Horse	nice but unrealistic	♥♥
Sheep	champagne and caviar	♥♥♥♥
Monkey	a colourful affair	♥♥♥
Rooster	worth persevering	♥♥♥
Dog	honest and sincere	♥♥♥
Pig	a prickly partnership	♥♥

COMPATIBILITY RATINGS:
♥ *conflict* ♥♥ *work at it* ♥♥♥ *strong sexual attraction* ♥♥♥♥ *heavenly!*

PIG + SHEEP
★ Plenty of understanding and
love make this a winning team.

PIG + MONKEY
★ Occasional strife heightens the
sexual tension between you.

PIG + ROOSTER
★ Despite your temperamental
differences, you two could really
make a go of this; it's worth it if
you do.

PIG + DOG
★ A solid, amicable but rather
unadventurous partnership.

PIG + PIG
★ Early mind-touch later palls.

*A Pig can
find lasting
contentment
with a
Sheep.*

Hot Dates

IF YOU'RE DATING someone for the first time, taking your partner out for a special occasion or simply wanting to re-ignite that flame of passion between you, it helps to understand what would please that person most.

RATS ★ *Wine and dine him or take her to a party. Do something on impulse... go to the races or take a flight in a hot air balloon.*

OXEN ★ *Go for a drive in the country and drop in on a stately home. Visit an art gallery or antique shops. Then have an intimate dinner à deux.*

'So glad to see you...'
COCA-COLA 1945

TIGERS ★ *Tigers thrive on excitement so go clay-pigeon shooting, Formula One racing or challenge each other to a Quasar dual. A date at the theatre will put stars in your Tiger's eyes.*

RABBITS ★ *Gentle and creative, your Rabbit date will enjoy an evening at home with some take-away food and a romantic video. Play some seductive jazz and snuggle up.*

DRAGONS ★ *Mystery and magic will thrill your Dragon date. Take in a son et lumière show or go to a carnival. Or drive to the coast and sink your toes in the sand as the sun sets.*

SNAKES ★ *Don't do anything too active – these creatures like to take life sloooowly. Hire a row-boat for a long, lazy ride down the river. Give a soothing massage, then glide into a sensual jacuzzi together.*

The Carnival
GASTON-DOIN 19/20TH CENTURY

HORSES ★ *Your zany Horse gets easily bored. Take her on a mind-spinning tour of the local attractions. Surprise him with tickets to a musical show. Whatever you do, keep them guessing.*

SHEEP ★ *These folk adore the Arts so visit a museum, gallery or poetry recital. Go to a concert, the ballet, or the opera.*

MONKEYS ★ *The fantastical appeals to this partner, so go to a fancy-dress party or a masked ball, a laser light show or a sci-fi movie.*

ROOSTERS ★ *Grand gestures will impress your Rooster. Escort her to a film première or him to a formal engagement. Dressing up will place this date in seventh heaven.*

DOGS ★ *A cosy dinner will please this most unassuming of partners more than any social occasion. Chatting and story telling will ensure a close understanding.*

PIGS ★ *Arrange a slap-up meal or a lively party, or cruise through the shopping mall. Shopping is one of this partner's favourite hobbies!*

*Detail from
Chinese
Marriage
Ceremony*
CHINESE
PAINTING

Year of Commitment

CAN THE YEAR in which you marry (or make a firm commitment to live together) have any influence upon your marital relationship or the life you and your partner forge together? According to the Orientals, it certainly can. Whether your marriage is fiery, gentle, productive, passionate, insular or sociable doesn't so much depend on your animal nature, as on the nature of the Animal in whose year you tied the knot.

IF YOU MARRY IN A YEAR OF THE...

RAT ★ *your marriage should succeed because ventures starting now attract long-term success. Materially, you won't want and life is full of friendship.*

Marriage Feast
CHINESE PAINTING

OX ★ *your relationship will be solid and tastes conventional. Diligence will be recognized and you'll be well respected.*

TIGER ★ *you'll need plenty of humour to ride out the storms. Marrying in the Year of the Tiger is not auspicious.*

RABBIT ★ *you're wedded under the emblem of lovers. It's auspicious for a happy, carefree relationship, as neither partner wants to rock the boat.*

DRAGON ★ *you're blessed. This year is highly auspicious for luck, happiness and success.*

SNAKE ★ *it's good for romance but sexual entanglements are rife. Your relationship may seem languid, but passions run deep.*

HORSE ★ *chances are you decided to marry on the spur of the moment as the Horse year encourages impetuous behaviour. Marriage now may be volatile.*

SHEEP ★ *your family and home are blessed but watch domestic spending. Money is very easily frittered away.*

Marriage Ceremony
CHINESE PAINTING

豬

29

MONKEY ★ *married life could be unconventional. As plans go awry your lives could be full of surprises.*

ROOSTER ★ *drama characterizes your married life. Your household will run like clockwork, but bickering could strain your relationship.*

DOG ★ *it's a truly fortunate year and you can expect domestic joy. Prepare for a large family as the Dog is the sign of fertility!*

PIG ★ *it's highly auspicious and there'll be plenty of fun. Watch out for indulgence and excess.*

Marriage Ceremony (detail)
CHINESE PAINTING

Detail from Chinese Marriage Ceremony
CHINESE PAINTING

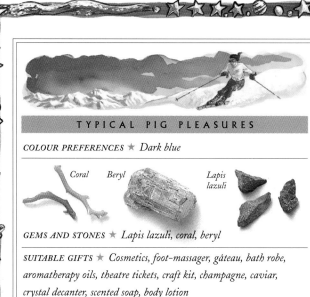

TYPICAL PIG PLEASURES

COLOUR PREFERENCES ★ *Dark blue*

Coral   Beryl   Lapis
                                  lazuli

GEMS AND STONES ★ *Lapis lazuli, coral, beryl*

SUITABLE GIFTS ★ *Cosmetics, foot-massager, gâteau, bath robe, aromatherapy oils, theatre tickets, craft kit, champagne, caviar, crystal decanter, scented soap, body lotion*

HOBBIES AND PASTIMES ★ *Shopping, amateur dramatics, ski-ing, golf, crosswords, dinner parties, flirting, opera*

HOLIDAY PREFERENCES ★
Holidays are made for Pig-born individuals – especially in five-star hotels. With your love of the easy life, lying on a sandy beach, soaking up the sun while sipping a long, cold cocktail is your idea of heaven.

COUNTRIES LINKED WITH THE PIG ★ *Denmark, Iceland, Israel, Brazil, Pakistan*

Vatnajokull Glacier, Iceland

The Pig Parent

TO BASK IN THE LOVE of a
closely-knit family is all that you
ask. In China, the Year of the Pig
symbolizes the home and family,
which means that you're a domestic
creature, at your happiest amongst
your loved ones and devoted to your
youngsters. You care for their every need, even go without
yourself in order to provide for them. Since you like an easy life
you believe in providing your offspring with a relaxed
environment in which they can grow and prosper.

*Pigs are
passionately
fond of
their
piglets.*

CULTURE VULTURE

You insist on politeness and good manners and because culture
and refinement are also important to you, you'll make sure you
take them to the theatre and museums almost from the moment
they're born.

THE PIG HABITAT

*Being a sensualist, chez vous is warm, deeply comfortable and
inviting. Impressing others is very important to you and this means
getting the décor just so, but you must guard against showiness. At
your most creative in your own home, you can turn the meanest shack
into a palace. But you can be a paradox – sometimes working until
you drop, sometimes so sedentary that an earthquake couldn't prise you
off the sofa. So though you create beautiful things, when it comes to
housework you may not be quite so assiduous.*

Animal Babies

FOR SOME parents, their children's personalities harmonize perfectly with their own. Others find that no matter how much they may love their offspring they're just not on the same wavelength. Our children arrive with their characters already well formed and, according to Chinese philosophy, shaped by the influence of their Animal Year. So you should be mindful of the year in which you conceive.

BABIES BORN IN THE YEAR OF THE...

RAT ★ *love being cuddled. They keep on the go – so give them plenty of rest. Later they enjoy collecting things.*

OX ★ *are placid, solid and independent. If not left to their own devices they sulk.*

TIGER ★ *are happy and endearing. As children, they have irrepressible energy. Boys are sporty and girls tom-boys.*

RABBIT ★ *are sensitive and strongly bonded to their mother. They need stability to thrive.*

DRAGON ★ *are independent and imaginative from the start. Encourage any interest that will allow their talents to flourish.*

SNAKE ★ *have great charm. They are slow starters so may need help with school work. Teach them to express feelings.*

豬

One Hundred Children Scroll
ANON, MING PERIOD

HORSE ★ *will burble away contentedly for hours. Talking starts early and they excel in languages.*

SHEEP ★ *are placid, well-behaved and respectful. They are family-oriented and never stray too far from home.*

MONKEY ★ *take an insatiable interest in everything. With agile minds they're quick to learn. They're good-humoured but mischievous!*

ROOSTER ★ *are sociable. Bright and vivacious, their strong adventurous streak best shows itself on a sports field.*

DOG ★ *are cute and cuddly. Easily pleased, they are content just pottering around the house amusing themselves for hours. Common sense is their greatest virtue.*

PIG ★ *are affectionate and friendly. Well-balanced, self-confident children, they're happy-go-lucky and laid-back. They are popular with friends.*

34

*Artistic
Pigs like to
get all the
details in
the frame.*

Health, Wealth and Worldly Affairs

ALTHOUGH YOU'RE GENERALLY ROBUST, your self-indulgence and a tendency towards sedentary habits can lead to health problems. Stomach and intestines are your vulnerable spots and you need to watch a tendency to put on weight. Loneliness or an unsettled lifestyle will play havoc with your system.

*Though you may lack
a competitive spirit,
shunning those jobs where
an element of
cut-and-thrust is
required, you are realistic
and know your own
strengths and weaknesses.
Once you've worked out
your aims in life, you'll go
flat out to achieve your
goal. Intelligence,
hard work, patience and
efficiency, these are
the qualities which
eventually win you
recognition and reward.*

CAREER

Adaptable and easy-going, you're suited to a wide range of occupations although you excel in the creative professions. You tackle jobs enthusiastically, always willing to help your colleagues. It's your attention to detail that earns you a reputation for fine workmanship.

Pigs are willing workers, but do best in a job that values their creativity.

FINANCES

It pleases you to spend money both on yourself and on others, for you're giving and generous to a fault. You have extravagant tastes and tend to go for the de-luxe model in whatever you're buying. Yet, despite such seeming profligacy, you can be canny where money is concerned.

Whether it's that you're prepared to work hard, or that you're shrewd in business, or have a good eye for a bargain or a nose for an investment, or even perhaps that you're just plain lucky, one way or another you'll end up nice and comfortably off.

FRIENDSHIPS

With your out-going disposition, a close social circle is important to you. You cherish your friends and love any sort of get-together. Good-natured and undemanding, you make many friends throughout your life and very few enemies.

PIGS MAKE EXCELLENT:

★ Students ★ Teachers ★ Researchers ★
★ Designers ★ Artists ★ Window-dressers ★ Florists ★
★ Actors ★ Entertainers ★ Craftworkers ★ Nurses ★
★ Doctors ★ Vets ★ Dentists ★ Dieticians ★ Hoteliers ★
★ Farmers ★ Butchers ★ Game-keepers ★ Caterers ★

THE
PIG

36

East Meets West

COMBINE YOUR Oriental Animal sign with your Western Zodiac birth sign to form a deeper and richer understanding of your character and personality.

ARIES PIG

★ *Full of* joie de vivre, *you're a warm friend and a lusty lover. Open and trusting, and optimistic in love, you believe that fidelity is an essential ingredient of a successful relationship.*

TAUREAN PIG

★ *You have a double helping of sensuality and buckets of charm and tenderness. You adore luxury, but you're realistic and have a good head for money.*

GEMINI PIG

★ *Witty and intelligent, you need variety in your life. Appearances are so important to you that you often fall in love with someone for the wrong reasons. Never judge a book by its cover!*

CANCERIAN PIG

★ *You are enormously generous and big-hearted. A born family person, you're idyllically happy around your own hearth. With your mega sex drive, it's odds on that you'll have a large family.*

LEONINE PIG

★ *Passionate and theatrical, you could be described as larger than life. You put one hundred per cent into everything and your high spirits are irrepressible.*

VIRGO PIG

★ *You're loyal and dedicated to those you love and would go without for the good of your family. But, if you're let down hell hath no fury like the Virgo Pig.*

豬

LIBRAN PIG

★ Beauty, creativity and refinement are components that you seek in your life, in your home and in your partner. Ideally, you would like to live a life of ease and comfort. Indecision sometimes slows you down.

SCORPIO PIG

★ Partners are advised never to cross you because of the sting in your tail! When you love, it's exclusive and you expect your partner to feel the same. Sex is high on your agenda and you attract suitors like bees to a honey-pot.

SAGITTARIAN PIG

★ A jovial, generous and genial personality such as yours gathers a large and faithful following. You dispense largesse to all and sundry, scattering optimism and good cheer to those around. Your ideal partner must be able to share both your humour and your philosophical view of life.

CAPRICORN PIG

★ You're industrious, responsible, realistic, a staunch upholder of values and tradition. You know what you want and you know how to get it. This applies as much to the man or woman in your life as it does to your worldly aspirations!

AQUARIAN PIG

★ Born under the dominion of the Aquarian Pig, you're bright and breezy, sociable and out-going. In your scheme of things, mind-touch and being on the same intellectual wave-length as your partner far outweigh sexual passion and strict fidelity.

PISCEAN PIG

★ Sensuality is at the core of the Pig nature but with this combination your tendency to indulge yourself in pleasures of the flesh is magnified. Being loved and feeling secure are fundamental to your well-being and you'll do anything in your power to keep a relationship alive.

豬

38

FAMOUS PIGS

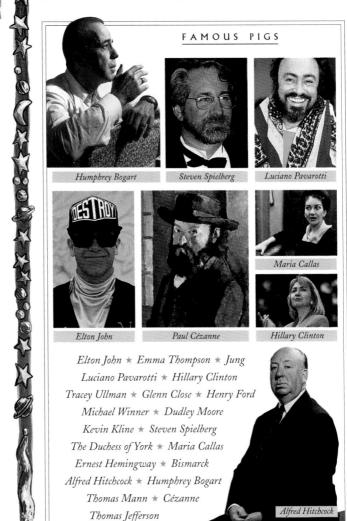

Humphrey Bogart   Steven Spielberg   Luciano Pavarotti

Maria Callas

Elton John   Paul Cézanne   Hillary Clinton

Elton John ★ Emma Thompson ★ Jung
Luciano Pavarotti ★ Hillary Clinton
Tracey Ullman ★ Glenn Close ★ Henry Ford
Michael Winner ★ Dudley Moore
Kevin Kline ★ Steven Spielberg
The Duchess of York ★ Maria Callas
Ernest Hemingway ★ Bismarck
Alfred Hitchcock ★ Humphrey Bogart
Thomas Mann ★ Cézanne
Thomas Jefferson

Alfred Hitchcock

The Pig Year in Focus

AS THE TWELFTH AND LAST SIGN of the Chinese horoscope, this year marks the end of the cycle. Concentrate on endings and don't start anything new. Affairs should be put in order ready for the new cycle.

39

OPTIMISTIC

This year there will be a decided sense of optimism in the air, with most experiencing some effects of the feel-good factor as the economy takes an upswing. It is a period of conspicuous consumption, a year for having a good time, for eating, drinking and enjoying ourselves.

Eat, drink and be merry – it's your year.

RECORD-BREAKING

The leisure industry does well, with luxury goods enjoying a roaring trade. Gambling reaches fever-pitch and records are broken in the world of sports. As the sign of the family, this year favours all domestic matters.

ACTIVITIES ASSOCIATED WITH THE PIG YEAR

The discovery, invention, patenting, marketing, manufacturing or formation of: vitamins, plastic, Kodachrome colour film, carbon 14, the transistor, the Rorschach ink blot test and Australopithecus.

豬

Your Pig Fortunes
for the Next 12 Years

1996 MARKS THE BEGINNING of a new 12-year cycle in the Chinese calendar. How your relationships and worldly prospects fare will depend on the influence of each Animal year in turn.

1996 YEAR OF THE RAT   *19 Feb 1996 – 6 Feb 1997*

Rat years herald fresh starts and new opportunities and this has a de-stabilizing effect on you. You prefer a settled atmosphere so the sense of shifting sands may disturb your peace of mind. Take heart, it isn't all bleak and you will win through.

YEAR TREND: THINK POSITIVE

1997 YEAR OF THE OX   *7 Feb 1997 – 27 Jan 1998*

A bright and hopeful year when your innate talents come to the fore. Although you should avoid financial risks, begin laying foundations for your future. Family life is happy but romance unstable.

YEAR TREND: FOLLOW YOUR INSTINCTS

1998 YEAR OF THE TIGER   *28 Jan 1998 – 15 Feb 1999*

The quickening pulse of the Tiger Year is not conducive to your laid-back nature so you could be confronted with many situations that will try your patience. Money and personal relationships are particular bugbears. People may not be trustworthy this year.

YEAR TREND: KEEP YOUR HEAD DOWN

1999 YEAR OF THE RABBIT | *16 Feb 1999 – 4 Feb 2000*

This year comes as balm to soothe your wounds. At work you progress by leaps and bounds; at home you feel much more settled and a good deal happier than of late. A time to celebrate and enjoy yourself.

YEAR TREND: ON THE UP

2000 YEAR OF THE DRAGON | *5 Feb 2000 – 23 Jan 2001*

One or two unusual events are likely to punctuate this year bringing highlights to an otherwise steady and settled twelve-month period. Socializing, attending cultural functions and maintaining a high profile will not only extend your network of contacts but will also attract valuable allies.

YEAR TREND: PLEASING PROSPECTS

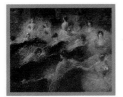

The Year of the Dragon will see many nights at the opera for socialite Pigs.

2001 YEAR OF THE SNAKE | *24 Jan 2001 – 11 Feb 2002*

Snake years are notorious for producing an atmosphere of uneasiness and disquiet which affects everyone in one form or another. For you, the focus falls on family affairs where scandal or loss may disturb the pattern of life. Expenditure needs to be controlled.

YEAR TREND: A TIME FOR TAKING STOCK

豬

2002 YEAR OF THE HORSE *12 Feb 2002 – 31 Jan 2003*

A busy year in which you can recoup losses and make steady headway. At work, past efforts will be rewarded giving you a sense of optimism and well-being. Family life will be pleasant and prosperous.

YEAR TREND: PLEASING RESULTS

2003 YEAR OF THE SHEEP *1 Feb 2003 – 21 Jan 2004*

Although at work progress is slow, Sheep years are auspicious times for love and marriage. Since you thrive in an atmosphere of domestic tranquillity and contentment, you should find that emotionally, 2003 will be immensely fulfilling and satisfying.

YEAR TREND: RELATIONSHIPS BRING HAPPINESS

2004 YEAR OF THE MONKEY *22 Jan 2004 – 8 Feb 2005*

Not the easiest of years for you mainly because you will find it hard to make ends meet. A lack of support from those around you adds to the feeling of an uphill struggle. Romance, however, lightens the load considerably, especially for new lovers.

YEAR TREND: MODEST GAINS

*Pigs must
be extra
diligent in
the Year of
the Rooster.*

豬

43

2005 YEAR OF THE ROOSTER *9 Feb 2005 – 28 Jan 2006*

It looks as if your money problems iron themselves out this year but you're warned not to take any financial risks. In business, progress could be erratic and there will be hurdles that require careful negotiation. Relationships will be prone to underlying tensions.

YEAR TREND: SWINGS AND ROUNDABOUTS

2006 YEAR OF THE DOG *29 Jan 2006 – 17 Feb 2007*

This year improves as it advances; early difficulties give way to later triumphs. Review your aims and objectives and plan for the future. An auspicious time for marriage, moving or starting a family.

YEAR TREND: IMPROVED CIRCUMSTANCES

2007 YEAR OF THE PIG *18 Feb 2007 – 6 Feb 2008*

This is your year when you can make excellent progress in many areas of your life. Plans put into motion last year come to fruition now and any residual domestic or relationship problems can be ironed out. The auspices are good for marriage or moving house.

YEAR TREND: HAPPY TIMES

PICTURE CREDITS